Dr Doodle

in

SANTALAND

Illustrated by

Louise M Hurd

DB

DORRIT BOOKS

Published by DORRIT BOOKS

Kettering
Northants
NN15 6JD

ISBN 0-9532296-6-1

I hope you enjoy reading this story.

Other books in this series:

Dr Doodle's VERSES

Dr Doodle in COMPUTERLAND

Dr Doodle meets BULBO DELIGHT

Dr Doodle's ANIMAL VERSES

It is Christmas Eve,
The night is cool,
Dr Doodle and four pupils
From his school
Are laughing and joking
And really carefree,
As they begin decking
The old oak tree.

With tinsel and baubles
And sparkling lights
This magical tree
Is a brilliant sight.
Now all that is needed
To make it complete,
Are presents for friends
And the odd chocolate treat.

"Wouldn't it be cool,"
Says Tom with a cheer,
"To invite our friends
To a party up here -
We'd give them presents
And pull crackers too,"
And all are agreed
It would be terrific to do.

SANTA!

"But where could we get
Lots of presents and gifts
At this time of night?"
Says Sue munching crisps.
"It appears to me,"
Says Tom with glee,
"The most likely source
Is Santa of course!"

"I have no doubt,"
Dr Doodle begins,
"That Santa would
Help us with
Presents and things.
But how do we get
To him at this time
Of night? That is
The question."
And he is quite right.

Then Sophie cries out,
To everyone's surprise,
"I wish Ollie the Owl
Was ten times his size -
Then he could fly us
Through the night sky
To visit old Santa
And give it a try!"

Since Sophie is in
The magical tree,
Her wish has come true
As all can see.
For there is old Ollie
Ten times his size,
With massive great wings
And big rolling eyes.

"Yippee!" shouts Jack,
Startling the rest.
"Come on, all aboard
The great owl express!"
Then one by one
They all clamber up,
Holding on tightly
To big Ollie's back.

Owl flaps his wings,
Creating some wind,
(Which wakes the birds
Who begin to sing):
Then off he zings
Into the night sky
Like a big aeroplane
That zooms very high.

Big Ollie glides
Into the night,
Amid the stars
That twinkle so bright -
The ride is smooth
And a sheer delight.

SANTA'S GROTTO
SANTA'S GROTTO

Soon Santaland
Comes into sight;
Covered in snow
On this cold night.
Then Santa's Grotto
Comes into view,
Shown in large letters
And lit up in blue.

SANTA'S GROTTO
SANTA'S
GROTTO

Owl touches down
On an icy track,
Where the scholar
And pupils
Slide off his back.
Then hand-in-hand
Through the snow
They all go,
Following a path
To Santa's Grotto.

Into the Grotto
They all make their way,
Except for Ollie
Who outside has to stay.
There they find Santa
With reindeer and elves
In a spacious room
With empty shelves.

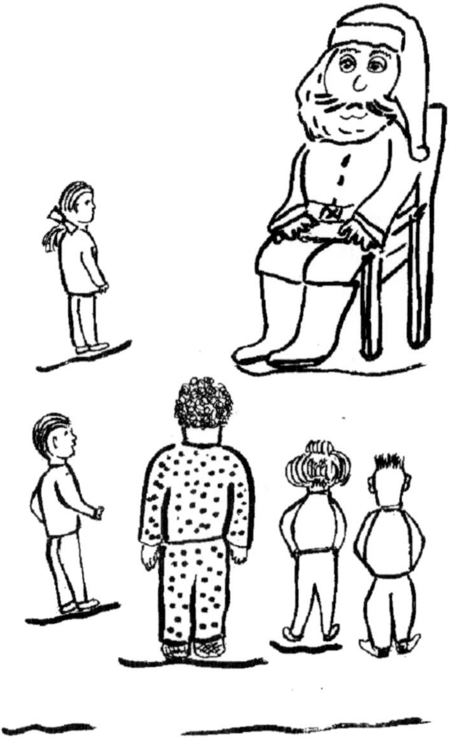

Santa welcomes them
With a look quite forlorn.
"Hello - who are you . . .
And where are you from?"
"I'm Dudley Doodle,"
The scholar says warmly -
"And these are my pupils
From Gorton-cum-Chormly."

"Excuse me," says Santa,
"If I'm not me tonight;
I'm feeling low
And not very bright."
When asked the reason,
He then replies:
"My sleigh has been stolen -
I'm really quite shaken:
My sacks full of presents,
Have all been taken."

They all feel sorry
For poor Santa's plight;
And so they say,
"Can we help you tonight?"
Then Santa replies
With hope in his eyes,
"If my sleigh and sacks
Could all be retrieved,
I would be most grateful
And mightily relieved."

What a predicament
For Santa to be in -
For no gifts or toys
Can now be given,
To girls and boys
On Christmas day
If nothing is done
Straight away.

The Grotto is filled
With doom and gloom:
A sorry state
For all in the room.
The elves are crying
The reindeer sulk;
All are hoping for
A stroke of good luck.

HOOT! HOOT!
WHOO! WHOO!
HOOT! HOOT!
TWIT-TWOO!

Then while everyone
Wonders what to do,
From outside the Grotto
Noises ensue -
Of "Hoots" and "Whoos"
And "Twit-Twoo",
It sounds as if Ollie
Is in a bit of a stew.

Going outside to see
What the matter can be,
They find owl
Behaving excitedly;
Hooting and flapping
And creating a scene,
Pointing to something
That he has seen.

The thing Ollie saw
Lies in the snow.
It makes no movement
But gives out a glow.
"It's a toy -" says Santa
With a loud shout.
"And it's one of mine,
Of that there's no doubt."

"But how did it get here!"
He cries out to himself.
"We do not know,"
Replies a fat dumpy elf.
So they follow a trail
Of presents and toys
Which leads to a cave
From which comes a noise.

Into the cave they
All make their way,
Except for Ollie
Who outside has to stay.
And what they see
They cannot believe,
For a very big snowman
Is in Santa's sleigh,
Holding a trumpet
And blowing away.

"Well bless my socks!"
Says Santa amazed.
"It's old Bigtoe
With my sleigh and sacks!
That horrible snowman
With no manners or brain."

"Bigtoe," Santa begins.
"You're a very bad snowman!
For all these things
Are not yours, you know man.
And to take them away
You know is not right,
When they have to be
Given to children tonight."

Bigtoe is sorry
(Or so he said),
But he only wanted
The toys to play
With in bed.

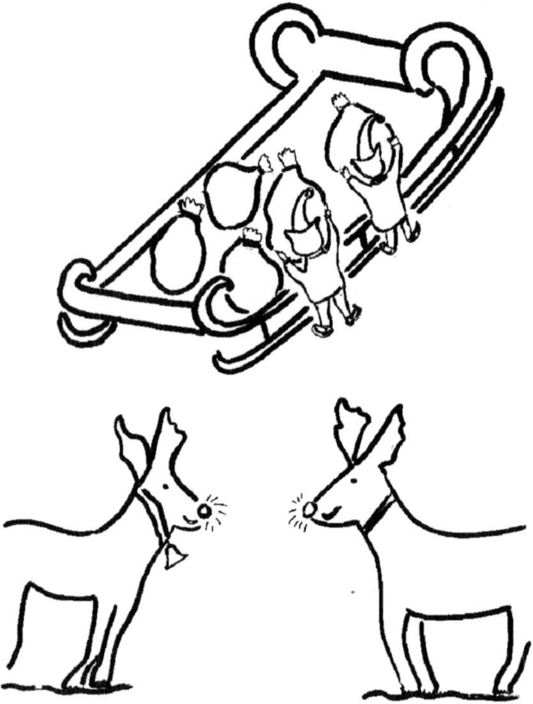

Santa forgives him
Then says to the elves:
"Come little friends,
Let's busy ourselves . . . "
Then giving a whistle
The reindeer appear
With noses aglow
And in very good cheer.

Harnessing the reindeer
Up to the sleigh,
Santa says to the others
As they watch this display:
"I'm afraid I must hurry,
We cannot delay,
Must deliver these presents
For Christmas day."

Another whistle is given
Then the sleigh pulls away.
But before taking off
Santa turns to say:
"My very dear friends
I'm glad that you stayed . . .
Please take this sack
For the part that you played."

"Goodbye Santa,"
The pupils call back.
"Great to have met you,
And thanks for the sack."
Then the reindeer and sleigh
Zoom into the night,
Over Santaland and Lapland
And then out of sight.

"What an adventure,"
Says Sophie with glee.
"We came to ask Santa
For gifts for our tree -
And got what we wanted
In a strange sort of way -
Thanks to big Ollie
Who saved the day."

Ollie flaps his wings
And hoots with delight,
For he knows that Sophie
Is certainly right.
But now it is time
To travel back home,
So they climb on his back
And off they all zoom.

Back at the tree
Old Ollie the wise
Is changed by a wish
To his original size.
Then with him helping
They deck the big tree
With all Santa gave them
So generously.

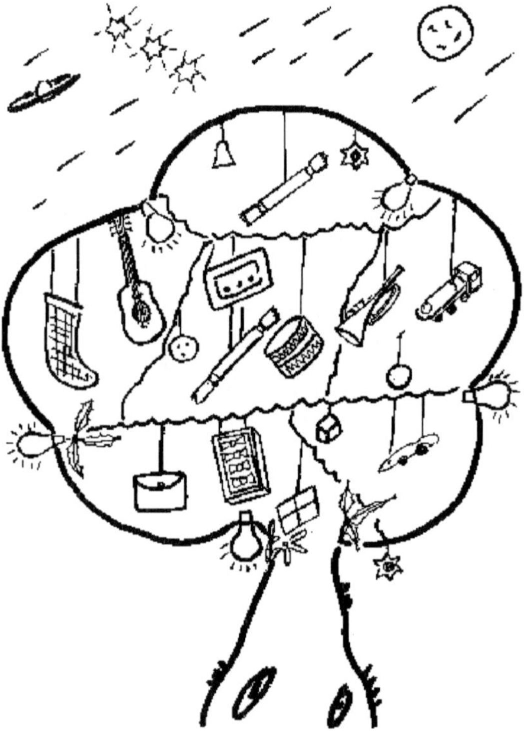

The work is complete:
The tree a fine sight:
Decorated with gifts
Each one a delight.
So thanks to old Ollie
And dear Santa too,
That party Tom spoke of
Can really come true!

See you again soon!